MARTIN BRANT

THE MONEY WILL FOLLOW

The Ultimate Guide on How to Monetize Any Industry, Discover Proven Strategies on How to Make Money Out of Anything and Set Up Profitable Income Streams

Descrierea CIP a Bibliotecii Naționale a României
MARTIN BRANT
THE MONEY WILL FOLLOW. The Ultimate Guide on How to Monetize Any Industry, Discover Proven Strategies on How to Make Money Out of Anything and Set Up Profitable Income Streams / Martin Brant – Bucharest: Editura My Ebook, 2021
   ISBN

MARTIN BRANT

THE MONEY WILL FOLLOW

The Ultimate Guide on How to Monetize Any Industry, Discover Proven Strategies on How to Make Money Out of Anything and Set Up Profitable Income Streams

My Ebook Publishing House
Bucharest, 2021

TABLE OF CONTENTS

Introduction 7

Chapter 1: **The Name of the Game** 9

Chapter 2: **Making Money Out of Anything…** *Anything!* 12

Chapter 3: **Why You Just Cannot Forget the Internet** 15

Chapter 4: **Build Something Successful** 18

Chapter 5: **Goodwill Hunting and Finding Niches** 21

Chapter 6: **Promoting Your Stuff Online – When Does the Confidence Come?** 24

Chapter 7: **The Power of Viral Marketing** 27

Chapter 8: **Building Your Battalion of Interested People** 30

Chapter 9: **Setting Up Streams of Residual Income** 33

Chapter 10: **Realizing the Power of 'I Can'** 36

Conclusion 39

INTRODUCTION

Monetization – the word has got a new meaning today. In these difficult times, people are trying to monetize just about anything and everything. Some are hitting the jackpot, achieving multiple monetization streams on a single product they have. While others are just wasting away, not quite able to come to grips with the concept of monetization.

Here is an eBook that tells you how you go about monetizing things. How you can add to your income putting in minimal effort, and ensuring that that income keeps on flowing into your bank account.

CHAPTER 1

THE NAME OF THE GAME

Summary

What is monetization? How are people doing it?

The Name of the Game

If you conduct some research on the Internet for what monetization actually means, you will be thrown up with a lot of definitions. Actually, monetization is an umbrella term for a lot of assorted things, but in a much generalized manner, we can say that monetization means making money out of things that people don't usually consider money-worthy. For example, if you have an old collection of Archie's Comics from your dad or your uncle and you are able to sell them for a tidy sum, you have monetized the collection.

Monetization means making money out of ordinary things, in unexpected ways.

It is quite easily understandable why people are going all out trying to monetize everything that is in their sight. Or, even out of sight. People are making money out of special talents that they have. If you have a special talent for math and are using it to tutor the neighbor's kid for money, you are monetizing your talent. If you are writing a piece of content and selling it to someone, you are monetizing your flair for writing.

We are all very conscious of monetizing, but have probably never done it in an organized manner. Our occupations pay us, and we are usually content with what we get and don't try to stick our necks out much. However, it is essential to know that there are several other things that we can make money out of. If we play our cards well, we can actually generate streams of passive income through things we set up once and enjoy the influx of money for our lifetime. That would be something like royalties on your products.

Monetization refers to what you can make money out of, over and above your usual profession. It is about your attempt, not the product's worth. It is about how you understand a particular thing or talent is monetizable and then how you go about it.

Here, we are going to see various methods in which you can build streams of income for yourself, out of things that you never felt you could make money from.

CHAPTER 2

MAKING MONEY OUT OF ANYTHING… *ANYTHING!*

Summary

Sounds desperate, but it is true. Rich people haven't become rich by undermining opportunities.

Making Money Out of Anything… *Anything!*

The first thing you have to realize when you are trying to develop the confidence to make money out of anything is this – *You can make money out of anything!*

But what is this 'anything' we are talking about? It could be a product that you have invented. If it has a utility – and sometimes, even if it doesn't – you can make money out of it. Or, it could be a product you have obtained from someone else and are now authorized to make money out of. Or, it could be a talent that you have. It could be simply your knowledge or some special knowhow about a particular thing.

Even people who think they have nothing have a lot of things they can make money out of. No one is wasting space here.

Before plunging headlong into discussions about how you can do this, let us speak about something very, very positive. *The Law of Attraction.* This law has gripped the world by storm and it is very much poignant to our topic of discussion. In a nutshell, the law says that – *When you think about something very strongly, the whole universe aligns itself to fulfill your desire.* Yes, the law states that thoughts bring results. It speaks about the energy of the mind, which can actually make things happen.

This is quite a true law, and people who have stated that the law is nonsense and doesn't work for them started with disbelief in the first place. If you want the law to work, you have to put your full faith in it. Think solely about your objective. Think about what you want. Think without flinching or hesitating. Slowly, things will start happening. When you think so deeply, you are bound to take actions in that direction. Everything that you do will be toward achieving that single goal. Naturally, things are going to start working out. Your deep, unwavering thoughts will bring you closer to the fulfillment of your desires.

Even when you are planning to monetize something, you have to put this law into action. Never for a moment must you think that there is no money in this. In fact, don't think in monetary terms, think of the larger picture. The money comes in as an aside. When you put in your efforts whole-heartedly, it doesn't take time for you to be rewarded monetarily anyway.

CHAPTER 3

WHY YOU JUST CANNOT FORGET THE INTERNET

Summary

The Internet is where the real monetization is at.

Why You Just Cannot Forget the Internet

Today, monetization has become almost synonymous with online businesses. People who want to make money out of anything will look at the Internet as their first and most significant domain of activity. There are many reasons why they tap the online resources for monetization.

First and foremost, today the whole concept of monetization has changed. No longer are people thinking conventional. They are trying to make money out of new ideas, new concepts, setting their minds to work. This is not possible unless these entrepreneurs can find the very people who have a liking for what they are selling. In short, they are working in specialized niches and that is the reason they need to find people who they can regard as their niche clientele.

The Internet allows that. When you are working on the Internet, you will find that there are tons of ways in which you can find people interested in whatever you are trying to do. You want to build a fan site for a show that no one watches around you? You can do that on the Internet. You want to speak about a hobby that you have and think no one else has? You will be surprised to find how many people share you special fondness on the Internet. Do you have a particular talent that you think no one cares about? On the Internet you will find a whole barrage of people who do. Or, probably you have made a product that no one around you finds useful. You will really be pleasantly surprised to see that you have a niche market for that product as well, on the Internet.

The main thing is that the Internet boosts your confidence. When you know that there are several people who are interested in the same things as you are and are also interested in what you are trying to sell, you become more confident about making that object or conceptualizing that idea and monetizing it.

The best part of it is that there is no rejection. Gone are the days when sellers had to peddle their wares to the customers; today with the help of the Internet, it is very much possible to bring interested customers to your door. If you are the shy introverted kind who shudders at the idea of being refused, the Internet is the place where you can market.

The great amount of resources that you can find on the Internet is the biggest draw, of course. There are ways in which you can bring people right at your door, waiting to buy whatever it is you are selling. This is what bolsters your confidence and inspires you about your enterprise, even if it doesn't do anything else for you.

CHAPTER 4

BUILD SOMETHING SUCCESSFUL

Summary

Your first step would be to build something popular that you can use as your monetization vehicle.

Build Something Successful

Almost everyone who is a fan of American Idol knows about the various fan sites it has spawned. Most of these sites started off as just fan sites, with no money equation in them at all, but then they got a mind-boggling amount of popularity, which led the makers of these sites to think that they could make money out of them as well, and that's how a huge monetization option was born.

The same happened with the Harry Potter franchise. Mugglenet.com, one of the almost-official Harry Potter fan sites wasn't commercial when it started out. It was just a place for people who loved the boy wizard to hang out and know more about him. But then it garnered an astounding amount of popularity and after that, who wouldn't think of monetizing?

In both these cases, people built something first, not even thinking about money, then made those things popular and then started making money from it. That means, it is actually not necessary for you to make something with money in the picture right from the start. You could even go in later and make money from whatever you have. The one thing that's needed is to monetize a product is to make it hugely popular.

On the Internet, it is quite easy to make things immensely popular. You have the tool of blogs at your disposal. Make a blog with Blogger.com (a free blogging resource) or Wordpress.com (a paid one) and then make it popular. Once your blog becomes popular – i.e. people visit it in large numbers – you can start monetizing it in various ways, such as selling eBooks through it or selling newsletter subscriptions or maybe even building a membership site down the line. Even if you don't want to go the whole hog, i.e. don't want to build a blog as yet, you could explore monetizing streams through options like social networking. Make your business (it is time we started calling this a business) popular by building communities, inviting people on them and giving them great information. When people start coming in, various avenues for making money automatically begin opening up for you.

CHAPTER 5

GOODWILL HUNTING AND FINDING NICHES

Summary

You have started on your monetizing journey. Now, what you need is people who will pay you money!

Goodwill Hunting and Finding Niches

If you don't target the right people, you will find monetizing anything to be a very much uphill task. After all, how could you make money out of your recipes if you don't find people who would be willing to spend in order to learn those recipes from you? You see the point – you need to find your niche.

One of the best ways to do that on the Internet is known as Search Engine Optimization, or SEO for short. Chances are that you will already have a modicum of knowledge about SEO if you are dabbling with Internet businesses. If you don't, here's what it means. SEO simply means pumping up your website (a blog is a website as well) for the search engines. This is really important because the search engines are through where people are looking for information. When someone wants to know about something, they type in a word or a phrase in a search engine like Google or Yahoo! or Ask. Then, they visit the links that show up. Usually, people only click on the links that appear on the first page and very few go even to the second page. Hence, it becomes very important for someone wanting to become famous on the Internet (and hence monetize something) to figure on the first page of any search engine.

Even if you don't have websites of your own, you could make posts on other people's blogs and forums and get a good fan following of your own. Many blog commentators get a lot of responses, thus building fan bases of their own. When they get such a fan base, they go right ahead and build their own blogs or websites and introduce these people to them. This could be a great way to find your niche and earn goodwill among them too, without putting in any investment of your own.

Another way is through article marketing. You could write articles about the subject that you are trying to monetize.

These articles could then be put up in places such as EzineArticles.com, iSnare.com, ArticleAlley.com, GoArticles.com, ArticleCity.com, etc. The best part of submitting your articles to such places if that these places are already popular with the search engines. Hence, if you were to submit some very informative articles here, you could get a large fan following for them. Also, keep in mind that the people who will stumble upon your articles will be people who are actually looking for some kind of information in that particular department.

CHAPTER 6

PROMOTING YOUR STUFF ONLINE – WHEN DOES THE CONFIDENCE COME?

Summary

Monetization happens only when you are confident about what you are selling.

Even a fruit seller has to be convinced that his oranges are good or no one would purchase them from him. But you are decidedly going to play at bigger stakes than mere oranges here.

Promoting Your Stuff Online – When Does the Confidence Come?

One of the chief ingredients that you need to sell anything is confidence. That is actually you are looking for. But when does the confidence come?

Your confidence may be present right from the start. When you look at a particular short story you have written or a video you have made explaining a particular way to make bouillabaisse, you might think quite positively that you can make money out of it. Well, you can – there are several ways to go about that. This is the starting point of confidence, but there is a long way to go still.

What you really need to know here is that initial confidence does not stay. What is really important is that your confidence needs to be consolidated. It has to be reinforced. And what reinforces your confidence? It is results that do.

When you see things really happening the way you want them to happen, when you see that you are actually getting the money that you had started out to get, your confidence begins building up.

But it is not just about the money. Results in any form could be instrumental in keeping you moving on. For some people, even a small comment on one of the articles they have written or a blog post that they have made could be enough inspiration to keep going ahead. Try that out. Write something on a blog about a subject of your passion. If you get a reply for that, you understand that at least someone was influenced to some extent by what you commented. It gives you the much-needed shot in the arm to work better.

It could be anything that could motivate you, any kind of result. It could be an increased number of visitors to your blog, it could be people commenting, it could be someone inviting you to a social networking group, it could be someone emailing you, it could be someone asking you something directly about the subject of your expertise... the list could go on. Or, most importantly and you could say ultimately, it could be someone who goes ahead and pays you for what you are trying to sell.

This is what really builds up your confidence. However, you must remember that you have to start out with a modicum of confidence. The ideal situation would be to have unshakeable confidence right from the start, but if that doesn't seem to happen, you could at least find your motivation in the glories that keep coming your way.

CHAPTER 7

THE POWER OF VIRAL MARKETING

Summary

There's nothing for an entrepreneur's confidence than people recommending their businesses to others.

The Power of Viral Marketing

Viral marketing has been essential all through the ages, but in the era of Internet marketing, it has put a whole new ring on things. Have you ever been told by a friend that a particular book was good to read and then you have ended up purchasing it and reading it? Or have you ever visiting a restaurant because of someone's recommendation? If you have done these things, then you already know what viral marketing is. Viral marketing is what happens when a user promotes a product to someone else in their circle.

Why is viral marketing so poignant to our topic of discussion? That's because if you are trying to monetize something, the best and the most economical way to do it is through viral marketing. Think about it – when someone promotes your business to someone else that they know, there's a much better chance that you will get a new buyer? Don't you become keener on something if someone you know uses and recommends it? It works that way for everyone.

But the most important thing is not the business that you get. It is the confidence that it creates in you. When you know that people are not just buying your product but are actually going all out and recommending it to others, it means that you are doing something right. You become happy that you are getting all these positive reviews and recommendations and you are pepped on to do better.

So, where can you virally market your things? Your blog is definitely the best place to do it. Make regular posts there. People will visit. Some of them will use your product. If they like it, they will recommend it to others. Some might do it on the blog itself. This really feeds your ego!

Or, you could use social networking sites. On most social networking sites, you could invite people to join a particular group. You could have a group for your own business. Call people here. When some of them use your product and start recommending your product, everyone in the community comes to know about it. Most significantly, you come to know about it as well. You become quite contented with the way things are going. Not only is money coming in, but you have produced a legion of happy people who you can be sure will be carrying on your product to other people.

Viral marketing is a really powerful tool because the conversion ratio is the highest here. However, the another important thing about it is that you get interested people recommending your product to other people who may be interested and your niche starts growing deeper because of that.

CHAPTER 8

BUILDING YOUR BATTALION OF INTERESTED PEOPLE

Summary

You are really set when you have a huge collection of people who are impressed with your product and help you in selling the product to more people through referrals or more.

Building Your Battalion of Interested People

It is quite understandable why you could have a much better success at monetizing your product of passion if you have a huge army of people to promote what you are trying to sell. With the various tools that the Internet has to provide, you can do this in a very simple manner.

Remember that when there are a lot of likeminded people working with you, the confidence comes by itself. These people are your confidence bank; when you see them pushing your product, you get more driven.

So, how do you go about building this army of people? One of the ways of doing this is through ***lead generation***. Lead generation quite simply means to get contact details of people who are even remotely interested in what you are trying to sell. Now, there are various ways to do it as well, but one of the cheapest and commonest ways to do this is by giving people some free gifts such as eBooks or newsletter subscriptions. You could promote these giveaways on your blog page itself and give them a download link. However, this download link won't directly take them to the giveaway page. It will take them through a squeeze page where they will be asked their email ids. People won't mind giving their email ids because they are getting something free for it. These email ids will then be in your kitty – you could use them to entice people in various ways about your business.

When people add themselves to your list, your job is to keep providing them quality information. It might happen that they get much impressed with your newsletters, eBooks or emails and they end up buying your product. When they like that, they become a part of your formidable battalion. They will not mind recommending your product to others.

The same applies when you are monetizing your content. When people read your content, you could ask them to add themselves to your *feeds*. When they do that, they will automatically get to know whenever you update the content. They will visit again. They could become part of your admiration society. Such people will then recommend you to others (you could speed that up by giving them an incentive, such as a free subscription or an eBook, etc.). Your army is now at work. It is promoting your business idea beyond its reaches.

CHAPTER 9

SETTING UP STREAMS OF RESIDUAL INCOME

Summary

Monetization should never be a onetime affair. It needs to be a consistent effort, which can keep bringing in the money.

Setting Up Streams of Residual Money

If you can monetize something once, you can monetize it again and again.

This is a very important truth, and it is more important on the Internet where it is really very much possible to make money out of something several times over.

The concept of residual money is at the root of this. First, let us see what residual money is. Residual money is money that keeps coming for something you did once. Authors who get royalties from their novels are earning residual income. They worked on the novel once and then they keep earning royalties out of its sales practically for their entire life.

You could do things the same way on the Internet. It is quite possible for you to have an eBook written, for example, and promote it on various places of the Internet. This eBook could be about something you wish to monetize, like your knowledge of how to play a six-string guitar the right way. You could write authoritatively and then promote this on your blog and on other affiliate sites. Soon enough, people will start downloading the eBook for payment, and as the stream of viral marketing begins to kick in, you will start getting more money generated for your purposes too.

Every blog that is made, every website that is created, every article that is written becomes a stream of residual monetization on the Internet. These are your footprints in the virtual world and you can just dig into these and keep earning money. You must have heard of Internet marketers becoming multimillionaires. Well, they didn't do so by putting in laborious efforts for everything, all the time. The way they did this is by monetizing their knowledge and expertise. Their efforts were onetime, their marketing efforts were considerable and that kept the ball rolling.

So, you must go out and spread yourself as much on the Internet as possible. Get acquainted with the concept of affiliate marketing and link exchange. This is how you can spread yourself thin over a larger virtual surface. This is what will make more eyes attracted to what it is that you are trying to sell and bring you a constant stream of money that you will be proud of.

CHAPTER 10

REALIZING THE POWER OF 'I CAN'

Summary

You cannot make money out of the hottest-selling product in the world if you aren't sure of your own capabilities.

Realizing the Power of 'I Can'

Confidence is at the root of everything.

Even if the biggest selling product of the world were given to you, and you were told to make money out if, you couldn't do that if you weren't confident about it.

So many franchises of McDonald's and Taco Bells have failed all over the world. Why did they fail? Was it because the product hasn't proven itself already? The real reason there was that the sellers weren't confident.

Every success stems from within you. We have got it all wrong so far. We speak about being at the right place at the right time. That is all well, but if you didn't welcome the opportunity when it passed by you, could you ever succeed in anything? Success comes from our realization and belief in ourselves that we can succeed. We have to shun the thought of debility and convert it into possibility.

So, you can make money out of the slogans you can write so well. You can make money out of the cakes you bake. You can make money out of the knowledge you have about hydraulic screws. You can make money out of your passion for Lost. All you have to do is to be confident that you can make money out of these things.

Begin by thinking that there are people out there who want, or probably even need, to know or have what you are trying to monetize. When you are fully convinced there is a veritable market, you become confident. You understand that now you have the people ready, you just have to give them the goods.

The actual giving can be done by so many online routes. It is the Internet that can bring this niche of people closer to you. It is the Internet that makes you so supremely confident about everything.

So, delve in the power of 'I can'. It really motivates you to monetize.

CONCLUSION

It is quite possible to make money out of scrap and junk if you set your mind to it. If there is something of real value, it is also possible to monetize it over and over again.

You must begin by creating the confidence within yourself that you can do that.

Possibly, that has happened by now.

Printed by Libri Plureos GmbH in Hamburg, Germany